Alien Swap

Story by Stan Cullimore
Pictures by Nick Schon

OXFORD
UNIVERSITY PRESS

Harry glanced at the clock beside his bed. It was five minutes to eight o'clock. His stomach made a strange rumbling noise. He turned over in bed and cuddled his cat, Freddy.

"Freddy, I'm starving," he grumbled. "I should have eaten more of my tea." He pulled a face. "But I couldn't. It was all covered in disgusting, smelly cabbage. Yuk! It looked like green sludge and I..."

Suddenly Harry stopped. He could hear a strange noise. It sounded like someone humming. It was coming from outside. He turned to look at the window.

"What was that, Freddy?" He frowned. "It wasn't my stomach, that's for sure!"

He climbed out of bed, still holding his cat, and went over to the window. The humming noise came again. It was definitely coming from outside.

"It sounds as if it's right outside the window," he whispered to Freddy, clutching him tightly.

Harry pulled back the curtain, peered out of the window and whistled in shock. There was something outside. It was spinning and hovering in the air.

"I don't believe it," whispered Harry. "It's..., it's...., it's a flying saucer!"

Suddenly the humming noise stopped. The flying saucer stopped spinning. It glided smoothly towards the window.

A ladder came out of the strange craft. It poked out like a steel tongue until it reached the window ledge. Harry held his breath expectantly. A door opened in the side of the shining saucer. A peculiar-looking head popped out of the door.

"It's an alien," gasped Harry. The alien waved.

"Hello, Harry," burbled the alien. "Can I come into your bedroom, please?"

Harry nodded. "OK."
He wanted to ask it how it knew his name, but he felt a bit dazed.

"Thank you." The alien stepped confidently out onto the ladder. Then it whooshed over to the window ledge. "Watch out," it burbled, with a grin.

Harry stood back from the window. The alien lifted up its arm and touched one of the red buttons on its laser wristband. The pane of glass in the window began to glow.

The alien quickly stepped through the glowing glass.

Harry stared at the glass. "That was amazing!"

The alien touched the red button once again. The glass pane stopped glowing.

The alien shrugged. "It's nothing." Then it smiled. "By the way, my name is Zeto." Zeto the alien held out a hand. Harry went to shake it. Zeto pulled a face.

"There's no need to be rude!" snapped Zeto.

"I was only going to shake your hand," replied Harry.

Zeto shuddered. "How disgusting. Where I come from we don't do things like that. We do this." Zeto took hold of Harry's ear and tugged it gently. "Now we have to change places," Zeto announced.

"What?" asked Harry.

"It's my homework," replied Zeto.

Zeto took out another laser wristband and placed it around Harry's wrist.

"I have to swap places with a human," said the alien. "I have to see what things they get up to on Earth, and you are off to the alien planet."

"What? How long for?" asked Harry.

"One week," replied Zeto.

"What if I don't want to swap places?" asked Harry.

"It's too late for that," Zeto grinned. "Zod is expecting you and I've pressed the green button. Look in the mirror!"

"Oh, no!" He had turned into an alien. He looked just like Zeto. "I look really weird," he cried. "I'm Harry the alien!"

"You don't look as weird as I do," snapped Zeto. "Look what has happened to me."

With that, Zeto the human pressed the red button on his wristband. The window pane began to glow again. Harry felt himself being pushed onto the window ledge. Like it or not, he was going to the alien planet!

"You won't be needing this," said Zeto. He took Freddy from Harry's arms. "Where I come from they use cats to scare badly-behaved children."

Harry clambered into the flying saucer. The door closed behind him with a hiss and he sat down. A computer screen in front of him flashed up:

Destination: Alien Planet

Enjoy your trip!

"Yeah, thanks!" muttered Harry as it set off. The flying saucer flew past the moon and the stars. But it kept on going. It flew deep into space. Harry meanwhile was deep in thought, wondering what surprises were in store on the alien planet.

At long last the flying saucer stopped. The door swooshed open. Harry peered outside.

"What on Earth is going on?" he wondered aloud.

An alien was coming towards him dragging a dustbin.

"This isn't Earth," said the alien. "It's the alien planet."

"So I see," said Harry weakly as he was whooshed down to the ground on a jet of air.

"You must be Harry. I've been waiting for you. I'm going to be your teacher for this week. My name is Zod. But you can call me Mr Daft!"

"Mr Daft? Er... OK, Mr Daft."

Harry grinned.

"Now then, Harry. Are you hungry? Shall we get you some tasty alien food?"

"Yes, please! I'm starv…" Harry stopped in mid-sentence as he wondered what 'tasty alien food' might be exactly. "Well, I mean, I am a little peckish," he admitted. "Can you tell me where I can find a café?"

"I've got a better idea," replied Mr Daft. "Why don't I take you there?"

"OK then," Harry smiled.

"Well, as an extra special treat – I'll let you ride in the bin," said Mr Daft. "In you get." So Harry climbed into the bin.

"Er, thanks – I suppose," he muttered.

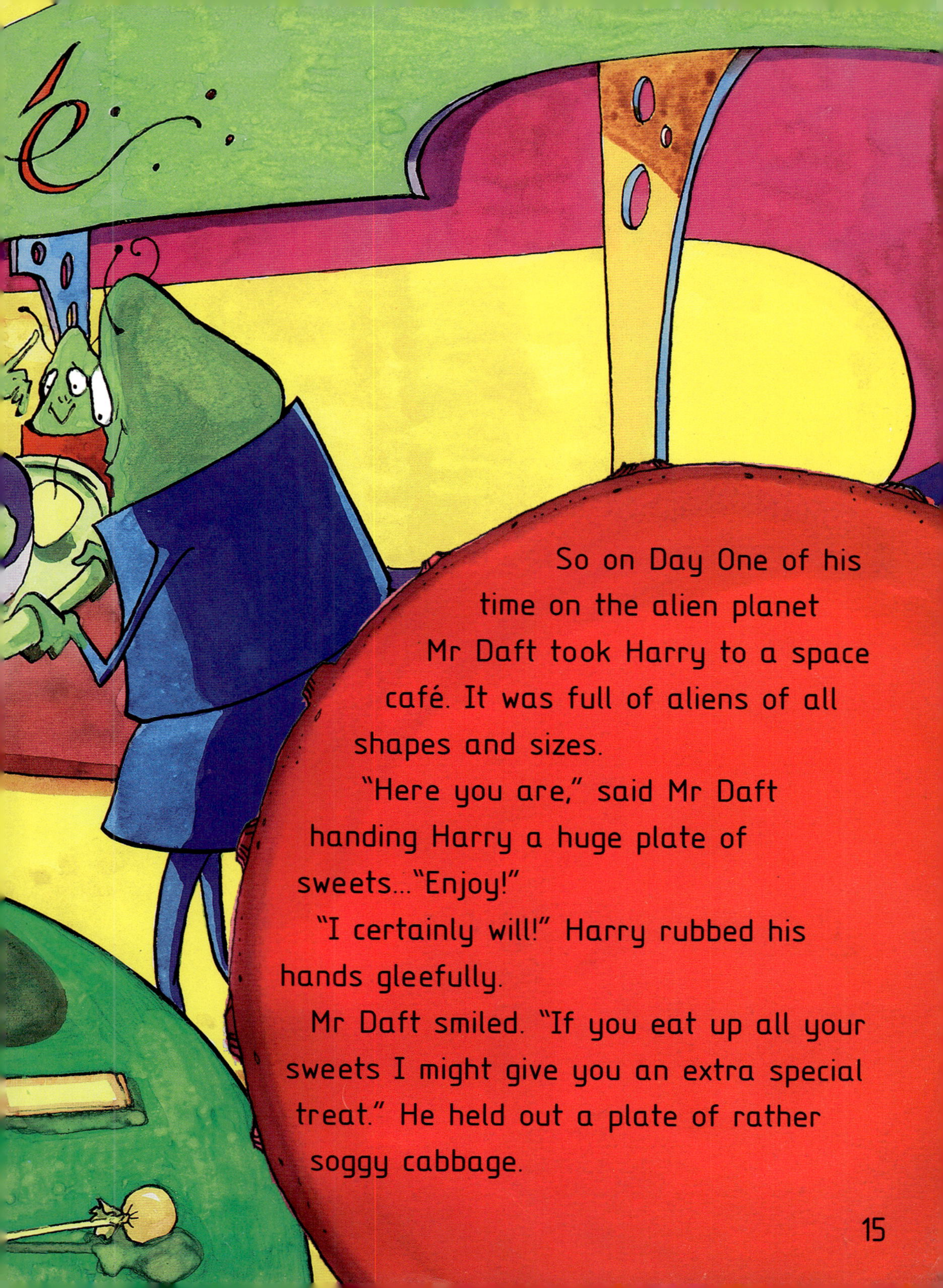

So on Day One of his time on the alien planet Mr Daft took Harry to a space café. It was full of aliens of all shapes and sizes.

"Here you are," said Mr Daft handing Harry a huge plate of sweets..."Enjoy!"

"I certainly will!" Harry rubbed his hands gleefully.

Mr Daft smiled. "If you eat up all your sweets I might give you an extra special treat." He held out a plate of rather soggy cabbage.

On Day Two, Harry went to alien school. The first lesson was PE.

"This is disgraceful," shouted Mr Daft. "Look at you. You are all disgustingly clean!"

So Harry and all the alien children had to climb into a jacuzzi full of green slime. It was cold and sticky and smelt a lot like a blocked drain.

Mr Daft sniffed the air and nodded happily. "Ah! That's much better."

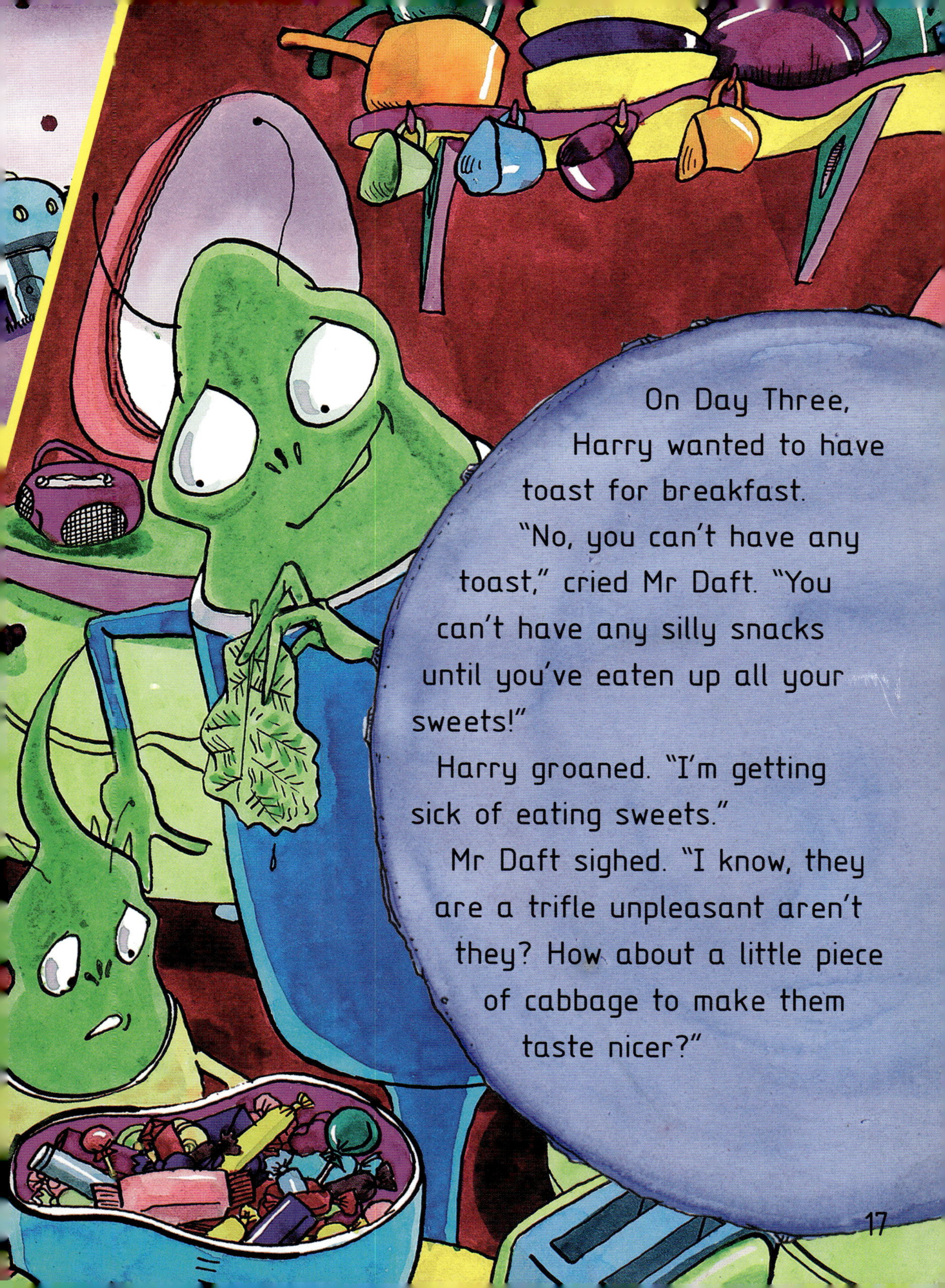

On Day Three, Harry wanted to have toast for breakfast.

"No, you can't have any toast," cried Mr Daft. "You can't have any silly snacks until you've eaten up all your sweets!"

Harry groaned. "I'm getting sick of eating sweets."

Mr Daft sighed. "I know, they are a trifle unpleasant aren't they? How about a little piece of cabbage to make them taste nicer?"

On Day Four, there was a school trip to a lunar space park. Harry thought it was fantastic. The first thing they did was to have a game of flying 'off-the-ground tig'. But for some reason the alien children were all extremely bored.

"Don't worry," said Mr Daft. "You don't have to play in the park all day. This afternoon, as a special treat, you will all be allowed to return to school. Then you can learn your times tables!"

The alien children all cheered.

On Day Five, Harry had a school dinner.

"Oh, no," he groaned. "Not again!"

The dinner lady had given him a huge helping of sweets.

"I never thought that I would get bored with eating sweets," moaned Harry. He had an idea. "Have you got any soggy cabbage?" he asked hopefully.

The dinner lady shook her head.

On Day Six, Mr Daft asked Harry how he was feeling.

"I feel fine," replied Harry. In fact he had a slight toothache, but he certainly wasn't going to mention that!

"FINE, you say? Oh, dear," frowned Mr Daft. "I think I ought to take you to the alien doctor."

"Why?" asked Harry. "I'm not ill."

"We aliens don't go and see the doctor when we are ill," laughed Mr Daft. "We go and see the doctor when we are feeling fine."

On Day Seven, Mr Daft sat Harry down. "Well, Harry, today you have to make a decision. You can stay here on the alien planet and eat up all these sweets..."

Harry shook his head.

"...or you can go back to Earth," added Mr Daft.

"Back to Earth, please," said Harry, quickly.

So Mr Daft put Harry back in the flying saucer. As he sat down the computer screen flashed:

Destination: Planet Earth

Enjoy your trip!

"Yes! Thank you!" cheered Harry as he was sent on his way.

When
Harry the alien
got back to Earth,
Zeto the human was
waiting for him.

"You live on a very
strange planet," said Zeto
the human.

"Not as strange as yours,"
said Harry the alien.

Zeto the human shivered.
"I can't wait to get back
to my old shape."

"Nor can I," agreed
Harry the alien.

They both smiled. Then they pressed the green buttons on their laser wristbands. Slowly, they both began to change into their old shapes.

"That's better," sighed Harry the human.

"Much, much better," added Zeto the alien.

Without another word, Zeto ran into his flying saucer. The door hissed closed and he flew away.

Harry went downstairs feeling very relieved to be back home. His Mum was sitting at the table.

"What's for tea, Mum?" asked Harry. "I'm starving."

"Sausages and mash," replied Mum. "And, there's some cabbage if you want any."

"Cabbage," cried Harry. "That sounds great! I just love cabbage!"